IGUANAS

Julie Murray

Big Buddy Books

An Imprint of Abdo Publishing
abdobooks.com

abdobooks.com

Published by Abdo Publishing, a division of ABDO, PO Box 398166, Minneapolis, Minnesota 55439.
Copyright © 2020 by Abdo Consulting Group, Inc. International copyrights reserved in all countries.
No part of this book may be reproduced in any form without written permission from the publisher.
Big Buddy Books™ is a trademark and logo of Abdo Publishing.

Printed in the United States of America, North Mankato, Minnesota
052019
092019

 THIS BOOK CONTAINS
RECYCLED MATERIALS

Design: Sarah DeYoung, Mighty Media, Inc.
Production: Mighty Media, Inc.
Editor: Liz Salzmann
Cover Photograph: Shutterstock
Interior Photographs: D. Parer & E. Parer-Cook/ardea.com (p. 27); Shutterstock (pp. 4–5, 6, 9, 11, 13, 14–15, 16, 19, 21, 23, 25, 28)

Library of Congress Control Number: 2018939825

Publisher's Cataloging-in-Publication Data
Names: Murray, Julie, author.
Title: Iguanas / by Julie Murray.
Description: Minneapolis, Minnesota : Abdo Publishing, 2020. I Series:
    Animal kingdom I Includes online resources and index.
Identifiers: ISBN 9781532116391 (lib.bdg.) I ISBN 9781532157882 (ebook)
Subjects: LCSH: Iguanas--Juvenile literature. I Iguanas--Behavior--Juvenile
    literature. I Reptiles--Juvenile literature. I Reptiles--Behavior--Juvenile
    literature.
Classification: DDC 597.9542--dc23

Contents

IGUANAS

Iguanas have been around for thousands of years. Iguanas are lizards. Lizards, snakes, and turtles are **reptiles**. Iguanas and other reptiles have **scaly** skin.

There are more than 30 kinds of iguanas.

Lying in the sun
is called basking.

Iguanas and other **reptiles** are **ectothermic** animals. Ectothermic animals lie in the sun to warm themselves. They cannot make heat inside their bodies.

WHAT THEY LOOK LIKE

Most young iguanas have bright green skin. Adult iguanas may be brown, gray, black, tan, or green.

Some iguanas match
their surroundings.
They can be hard to see.

9

Iguanas may be different sizes. Chuckwalla iguanas are about 15 inches (38 cm) long. Common green iguanas can be six feet (2 m) long.

The common green iguana is
also called the American iguana.

Iguanas have five toes on each foot. Each toe has a sharp claw. Some iguanas have rows of **spines** down their backs. The round spot behind an iguana's eye is its ear.

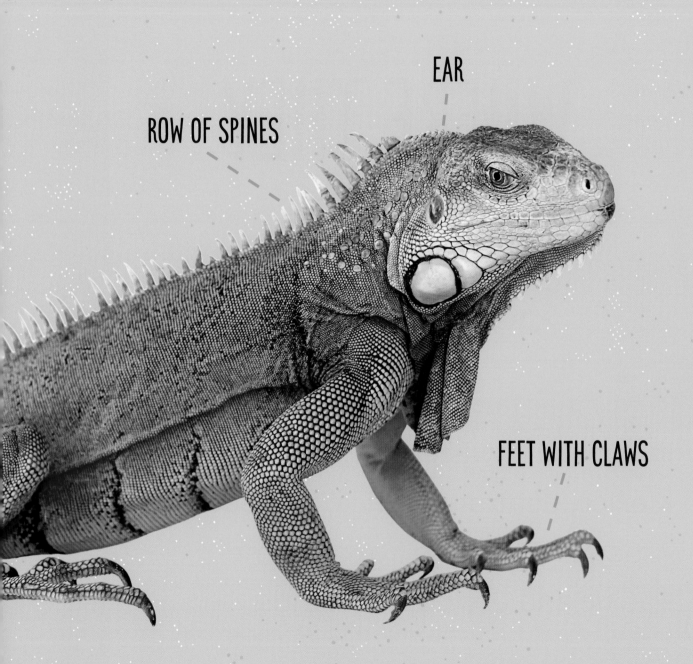

ROW OF SPINES

EAR

FEET WITH CLAWS

WHERE THEY LIVE

~~~~~~

Iguanas favor hot places. They live in the southwestern United States, Mexico, Central America, and South America. They also live on some Pacific and Caribbean islands.

The rhinoceros iguana lives on the island of Hispaniola in the Caribbean Sea.

A marine iguana can stay underwater for up to an hour.

Some iguanas live in the dry desert. Other iguanas live in forests. Some iguanas mostly live on the ground. Common green iguanas mostly live in trees. **Marine** iguanas spend time in the water.

WHAT THEY EAT

Iguanas look for food during the day. Iguanas eat leaves, fruits, and vegetables. **Marine** iguanas eat **seaweed** and **algae**. Iguanas that live in the desert eat **cactus** leaves.

Iguanas eat flowers too.

Pet Iguanas

Keeping a pet iguana is not easy. Iguanas grow very fast. Common green iguanas need a big, tall cage. They need branches for climbing. Pet iguanas need to warm themselves under special lights. Iguanas need sunshine too. Leafy green vegetables are good foods for iguanas. Iguanas also eat fruit. Pet stores sell special food for iguanas too.

GUARDING AGAINST ENEMIES

>>>>>>>

Wild cats and dogs, snakes, and other lizards hunt iguanas. Iguanas often run away from their enemies.

Hawks sometimes eat young iguanas.

23

Some iguanas run to water and swim away. Some climb trees. Others may hide under rocks or logs. An iguana can fight enemies with its tail and claws too.

Iguanas often lie on branches over water. They can dive in for a quick escape.

BABY IGUANAS

Most female iguanas dig a nest for their eggs. An iguana nest is a hole in the ground. Iguanas can lay as many as 50 eggs at a time.

A mother iguana covers her eggs with dirt and leaves. It takes many weeks for iguana eggs to **hatch**.

Female iguanas use their back legs to dig nests.

A baby iguana has a special egg tooth that helps it break out of its egg.

Newly **hatched** iguanas may be about 10 inches (25 cm) long. Mother iguanas do not take care of their babies. Baby iguanas must learn to live on their own. Iguanas can live to be 20 years old.

Glossary

algae (AL-jee)—plants or tiny plantlike organisms that live mainly in water.

cactus—a plant with sharp spikes that grows in hot dry places.

ectothermic (ehk-tuh-THUHR-mihk)—of or related to animals that cannot make heat inside their bodies.

hatch—to be born from an egg.

marine—having to do with the sea.

reptile—a member of a group of living beings. Reptiles have scaly skin and are cold-blooded.

scaly—having an outer covering made up of flat plates.

seaweed—plants that grow in the sea.

spines—a hard, sharp growth on a plant or animal.

Online Resources

Booklinks
NONFICTION NETWORK
FREE! ONLINE NONFICTION RESOURCES

To learn more about iguanas, please visit **abdobooklinks.com** or scan this QR code. These links are routinely monitored and updated to provide the most current information available.

Index